INSIGHT HERITAGE GU

THE PREHISTORIC TEMPLES AT KORDIN III

Kordin

NICHOLAS C. VELLA

PHOTOGRAPHY
DANIEL CILIA

HERITAGE BOOKS

and
FONDAZZJONI WIRT ARTNA
for
Cambridge University (TEMPER project)
2004

ACKNOWLEDGEMENTS

In different ways, various people and institutions have helped in the production of this guidebook and my sincere gratitude goes to all: Charles Borg, Jonathan Borg, Daniel Cilia, Mario Coleiro, Roberta De Angelis, Suzannah Depasquale, Louise Doughty, Ian Ellis, Mario Farrugia, Mario Galea, Chris Gemmell, Reuben Grima, Emmanuel Magro Conti, and Theresa Zammit Lupi.

Anthony Bonanno, Anne Chowne, and Richard Reece agreed to scrutinize the text when it was in draft form, pointing out infelicities and errors, and suggesting improvements. For this, and for their encouragement, I would like to thank them. Joseph Mizzi and John Busuttil kept calm every time I appeared at Midsea Books and presented them with tight deadlines, probably because this was, in a sense, a reversal of roles.

My sincere thanks go to the University of Malta for the research leave-of-absence granted to me on several occasions during the time that the TEMPER project was running. Finally, to Joseph Magro Conti I owe the invitation to take part in the TEMPER project and to bring me in touch with the sterling work done by non-governmental organizations in Malta. The stimulating discussions we have had at airports, trains, and bus stations, whilst waiting to be ferried to different parts of Europe and the Mediterranean to meet the rest of the TEMPER team, inspired me to look afresh at prehistoric sites and to write this guidebook.

This work is dedicated to my teachers, past and present.

Photo and illustration credits
The author and the publisher would like to thank the following individuals and organizations for the reproduction of some photographs that appear in this publication.

Albert Ganado collection p. 15
Malta Maritime Museum (Heritage Malta) p. 16

Mapping Unit, Malta Environment and Planning Authority p. 4 middle
National Museum of Archaeology (Heritage Malta) p. 6 bottom, 7 top, 13 top.
National Library of Malta p. 14 bottom
The Antiquity Trust p. 24
The British School at Rome p. 8-9
University of Malta Library p. 22

Insight Heritage Guides Series No: 5
General Editor: Louis J. Scerri

Published by Heritage Books, Carmelites Street Sta Venera HMR 1, Malta and Fondazzjoni Wirt Artna for Cambridge University

Insight Heritage Guides is a series of books intended to give an insight into aspects and sites of Malta's rich heritage, culture and traditions.

Produced by Mizzi Design & Services Ltd
Printed by Gutenberg Press

First published 2004
ISBN: 99932-39-86-0
ISBN: 99932-39-87-9

INTRODUCTION

Amongst the rich array of historical sites and monuments cared for by *Fondazzjoni Wirt Artna (FWA)* on behalf of the nation, the Kordin III temples hold a very dear place for all of us, especially those who like myself have helped to found and shape our trust to what it is today. For this site was, indeed, our very first undertaking, which takes us back to the early formative years of the trust, in 1987.

Our first involvement with this site was that alongside the now defunct Museums Department, when our volunteers dedicated numerous weekends to its upkeep. Since then we have moved on to obtain full responsibility for its conservation and management. It is our intention to provide full accessibility to this site on a regular basis, and this not simply by opening it up, but perhaps more importantly by providing the visitor with all possible means of interpretation that will help him/her experience to the full the rich history and unique characteristics of the site.

This guidebook is, therefore, one of the steps in that direction. It is produced as part of the Euromed Heritage II TEMPER project that ran from 2001-2004. TEMPER (an acronym that stands for 'Training, Education, Management and Prehistory in the Mediterranean') is a collaborative project involving six partner institutions and five archaeological sites in four countries spanning the European Union and the southern Mediterranean. The goal of the project has been to strengthen the concept of a common Euro-Mediterranean heritage using our shared prehistory.

The practical work of the project has resulted in the preparation of a management plan for all the prehistoric sites, including Kordin III, which will be implemented over a five-year period. It envisages the setting up of a visitors' centre on site to improve public enjoyment and understanding of the prehistoric monument, and to act as a first stage in a trail of heritage sites that *FWA* holds in trust in the Cottonera area. Moreover, as part of the TEMPER project educational pilot programmes have been devised in order to encourage a greater understanding of the importance of prehistory in developing thinking skills in children.

To my knowledge, this is the first attempt where all known information about this prehistoric site is being put to print in both an integral and fresh analytical way. Credit goes for this to the author Dr Nicholas C.Vella B.A. (Hons), Ph.D. (Bristol), lecturer in Archaeology at the Department of Classics and Archaeology at the University of Malta and to Joseph Magro Conti B.A. (Hons), M.A. (York), both of whom are trustees of *FWA*, for their unstinting efforts in clearing the mist of time about this important component of our national heritage. The way that this publication is being presented is, indeed, synonymous with our dictum as a society in making heritage knowledge as colourful and appealing as possible. I am confident that the effort involved in producing this guide book will be appreciated and enjoyed by all and sundry, whether they belong to the academic world or simply nurture an interest in the great curiosities of the past that this fair land of ours abounds so much with.

Mario Farrugia
Chairman & C.E.O.
Fondazzjoni Wirt Artna

LOCATION

Gozo

Malta

Valletta

Floriana

Kalkara

Hamrun

Birgu

Ras Ħanżir

L-Isla

Bormla

Kordin industrial estate

Kordin III •

Marsa

Paola

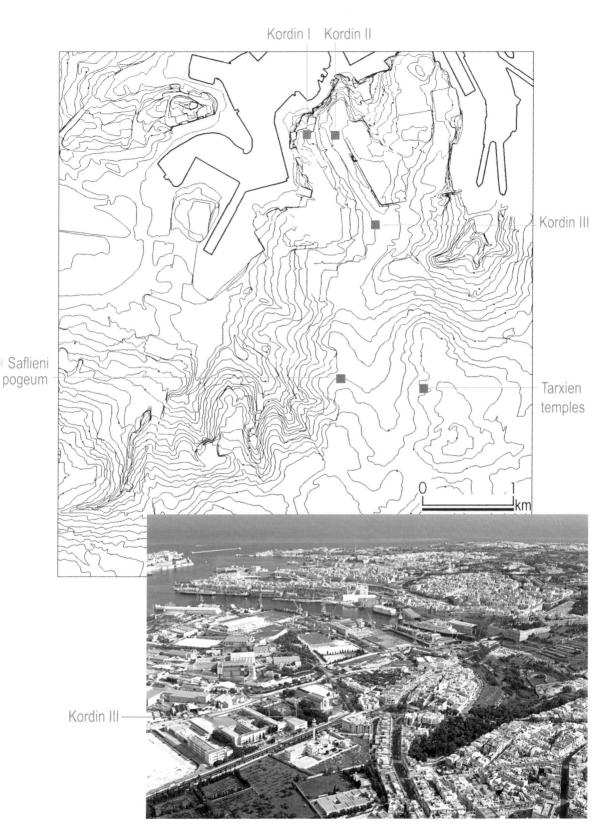

Kordin I   Kordin II

Kordin III

Saflieni
pogeum

Tarxien
temples

0   1
km

Kordin III

THE DISCOVERY OF THE SITE

**Ashby's plan of
Kordin I megalithic
remains**

The megalithic monuments of
Malta and Gozo have been a
source of bafflement and
fascination for antiquarians and
archaeologists for several
centuries. Visitors on their Grand
Tour of the southern
Mediterranean came to the
islands to look in awe at these
unique monuments from
antiquity. It was only during the
twentieth century, however, that
archaeological excavations
yielded reliable information about
their history and their age.

It is unknown when the
megalithic monuments on the
Kordin promontory were noticed
by visitors and locals for the very first
time. The earliest archaeological
probings seem to have occurred in

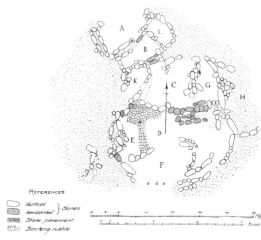

REFERENCES.

Vertical } Stones.
Horizontal
Stone pavement
Backing rubble

**Kordin I megalithic
remains, about 1890**

1840, the same year that the
megalithic ruins at Mnajdra were
being cleared, but the work at Kordin

ships in harbour

Floriana fortifications

was not continued. Several years later, the Public Librarian Cesare Vassallo cleared from debris a cluster of stone structures that he noticed close to the edge of the Kordin promontory, in shallow fields overlooking the Grand Harbour. In a guidebook to Malta's antiquities, he wrote in 1876 that he had uncovered stretches of curvilinear walls below five feet of soil. These were the same remains that the English naturalist Andrew Leith Adams visited during his sojourn in Malta between 1860 and 1866.

Between May and December 1892, further explorations of the same stone structures were conducted by Dr A. A. Caruana, at the time in charge of all archaeological explorations on the Maltese islands. Caruana's survey

Kordin II megalithic remains, about 1908

Ashby's plan of Kordin II megalithic remains

of the promontory revealed the existence of five groups of megalithic monuments, two of which were promptly excavated and a plan of each published. The first, Kordin I, lay on a terrace on the west slopes of the hill, at its tip, overlooking the Marsa plain. It consisted of the remains of several small contiguous enclosures. The eastern group, Kordin II, lay on the northern extent of the plateau, right on the summit of the ridge above Ras Ħanżir and 137 metres from the first group. A portion of the monument was destroyed when a ditch was cut in 1871 by the Royal Engineers to surround the military barracks nearby, but enough was visible for Caruana to identify the remains of a series of oval rooms that resembled those of the megalithic temple complexes at Ħaġar Qim and Mnajdra. The location of the remaining three groups of megalithic monuments that Caruana saw is unknown. Sadly, both Kordin I and II were already untraceable in the 1950s and the decision to turn the area in an industrial estate in the 1960s sealed their fate. Only some photographs, together with survey

excavations in process at Kordin III, June 1909

crate for pottery

awning

local workers digging

Cottonera – Marsa road

plans drawn for A. A. Caruana and updated by the German archaeologist Albert Mayr survive as testimony of these ancient remains.

The first true archaeological work in the area took place in 1908 by the curator of the Museum Dr Themistocles Zammit, and again between the end of May and June 1909 when Dr Thomas Ashby of the British School at Rome and his associates resurveyed Kordin I and II and carried out further excavations on behalf of the Government of Malta. A large mound of earth and large blocks that lay south of a road leading to the naval prisons from Marsa was also excavated. A large building similar in its trefoil plan to other known megalithic temples of Malta was uncovered together with a cluster of enclosures. The prehistoric site that became known as Kordin III was enclosed by a boundary wall at the end of the excavation. New research was only carried out in 1953 and in 1961 by the archaeologists Dr John Evans and Dr David Trump respectively for the purpose of dating the monument and checking the pottery sequence.

Archaeologist Thomas Ashby

Paola Civil Prisons

"trough"

TOUR OF KORDIN III TEMPLES

Today's visitor approaches the prehistoric complex from the east side through a gate in the site enclosure wall by the parvis of the Capuchin church. The entrance to the two adjoining temples is marked by a deep concave façade that overlooks an open forecourt, facing south. The temples are entirely constructed from the soft Globigerina limestone that outcrops in the area, with one noteworthy exception.

The temples' forecourt is beautifully paved in stone slabs of irregular shape set above a bedding of small cobbles resting on bedrock. The façade is built of a row of large megaliths with footing blocks in front. It has been partly reconstructed from blocks found by archaeologists lying on the paving in front. In the left-hand half of the façade, two neatly-worked stone slabs broken off at the top mark the doorway to the western temple. Unfortunately, here as elsewhere on the site, the lintels of the individual doorways have not survived. A paved passage or corridor lined with four stone slabs on either side leads from the forecourt to a spacious central court, paved too at the same level. The discovery in the doorway of a stone pounder of triangular form pierced with a round hole was reported by the archaeologists. Of particular note are the three stone slabs set on edge right across the passage, forming raised sills, the outermost being substantially higher than the rest. Anyone entering the temple from the forecourt, now as in the past, would have to exercise caution.

From the trapezoidal court that broadens towards the interior three semi-circular rooms or open apses in trefoil fashion. A low wall and a step – probably a later alteration discussed on p. 18 – separate the end and right-hand apses from the court. The floor of the latter room was made from *torba*, a hard plaster-like material made by the repeated pounding and wetting of several layers of Globigerina limestone dust spread over a rubble foundation. A substantial part of the semi-circular wall of this room was reconstructed

The temple complex facade showing the paved forecourt and the sills across the temple entrance

torba flooring

upright
megaliths

An aerial view of the
temple indicating the
various features found
within. *Left:* a plan of
Kordin III, the blue spots
mark the same features of
the photo below. To the
right of the blue line
marked 'A' to 'B' is the
angle of the panoramic
view of the temple as
shown overleaf

A

B

paved forecourt

facade

niches

sills

sill

'through'
(quern/boat model)

two-apse
temple

paved
court

infill

cross
wall

outer
wall

sill

three-apse
temple

areas of
torba

possible
hut foundations

by the archaeologists from the clutter of megaliths found lying on its floor.

The left-hand apse is divided into two by a straight wall. Its northern half is shut off from the court by a remarkable stone 'trough' placed between two massive pillar stones and behind a slab that rises above the paved floor of the court. The 'trough' is made from a single block of hard Coralline limestone – probably brought here from a source that outcrops a kilometre away near Żabbar – hollowed out into a series of compartments, separated from each other by thin partitions. Access to the southern half of the apse is through a constructed doorway, flanked on each side by three pillar blocks. Again, a low sill marks this otherwise level threshold that led to a *torba* floor. Sadly, the floor no longer survives. Against the curved wall of this apse are two niches formed by upright slabs and pillar stones. In a layer of soil above the floor, the archaeologists recovered a large quantity of potsherds, animal bones, and flint tools, the significance of which will be explored in later sections of this guidebook.

The apse at the end of the court opposite the temple entrance is entered through a regularly formed doorway set midway in the low cross-wall. Traces of *torba* flooring above bedrock were noticed beyond the threshold slabs and the usual raised sill. The archaeologists found a small round limestone button lying on the floor, together with a pear-shaped mace head, perforated at the smaller end. The walls of the apse are similar to ones elsewhere, but here a small

A panoramic view of Kordin III

niche or chamber, found full of pottery, was constructed within.

The eastern temple is accessed from a second doorway set in the façade. The remains here are less impressive mostly because the megaliths were broken up to build a lime-kiln within the temple area in more recent times. Beyond the constructed entrance, two contiguous apses or chambers, one larger than the other, define the temple's internal space. Only small patches of *torba* flooring were noticed by the archaeologists, the rest being bare rock. Of note are rope holes, one cut through the megalith flanking the entrance on the left-hand side, and another on one of the blocks in the wall of the right-hand apse.

Back at the forecourt, the wall that once surrounded the temples can be followed beyond the façade behind the eastern temple but not so much beyond the western temple where a chamber, separate from the rest of the complex, survives. The wall stops abruptly beyond both temples to the north. Instead, the remains of a number of enclosures defined by the traces of *torba* flooring and stretches of low walls visible during Ashby's excavation can be made out. These room or hut foundations probably belong to a village that existed on site before the temples were built. Where people lived when the temple complex was in use is unknown, no traces of domestic huts having been reported during construction works in the environs. The areas flanking the nearby valley, Wied Blandun, would have served the purpose. It is likely that the same people were buried in the communal cemetery known as the Ħal Saflieni hypogeum, about a kilometre away from Kordin III.

Overleaf:
The 'trough' in the central court of the western temple

THE HISTORICAL DEVELOPMENT OF THE LANDSCAPE

Standing in the forecourt outside the temples, surrounded by a boundary wall that has probably saved Kordin III from destruction, it is hard for the visitor to appreciate the wider physical setting of this prehistoric site. The landscape that we see today is the product of a series of major changes mostly induced by human action in connection with the Grand Harbour and its dockyards.

Until 1848 when the British inaugurated the first dry dock in Vittoriosa Creek, the Kordin promontory seems to have been very much a barren area with terraced fields on the slopes to the east and west and a racecourse for horses on the summit. The hydrographic chart of the Grand Harbour and its environs prepared by Captain William Smyth for the Admiralty in 1822 gives us an idea of the topography of the promontory before it was altered in the second half of the nineteenth century. Three ridges of Globigerina limestone met at the

neck of the promontory. To the north and east, a minor escarpment defined the edge of the promontory, with views across to the Valletta peninsula and French Creek respectively. Between two of the ridges, a narrow valley climbed up from the shore at Ras Ħanżir. Kordin III lies on the knoll of the westernmost ridge overlooking Wied Blandun and the

Aerial view of Kordin III temple complex surrounded by a wall, 1925

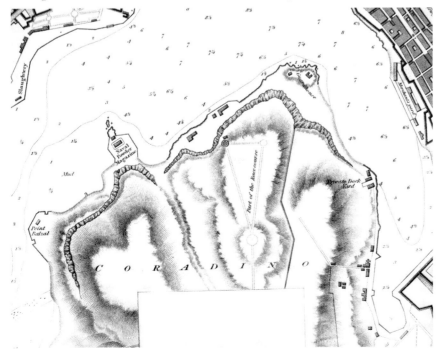

W.H. Smyth's survey (1822) of the Kordin promontory before major transformations in the British period

15

higher lands of
Paola and Tarxien
further south.
Kordin I and II lay
600 m to the north
of Kordin III on
the same ridge: the
first on its western
slopes overlooking
the low-lying
alluvial plains of
the Marsa at the
head of Grand
Harbour, the
second nearby but
higher up on the
summit, overlooking the harbour and
the valley that linked the uplands
with the sea below.

In prehistory, when the temples of
Kordin III were being used, the basic
landform of the Grand Harbour area
would have been similar to the
existent one. It is still unclear what
type of covering would have
characterised the Maltese islands in
prehistory. Substantial tree cover on

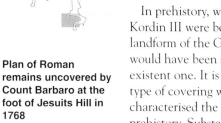

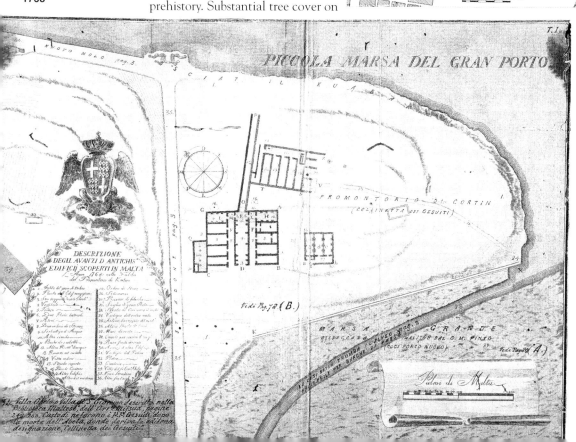

much of the land surface is assumed by archaeologists for and until the end of the Neolithic period (about 2500 BC) but this awaits confirmation. The sea must have extended much farther inland in antiquity than it does now in the Marsa area, turning the inlet here into a veritable harbour or anchorage in a way that the main expanses of the Grand Harbour and Marsamxett, too exposed for early shipping, did not. The eighteenth-century discovery and excavation of a complex of Roman warehouses, some stacked with amphorae ready for export, at the foot of Jesuits Hill right across the sea from Kordin (below the present Power Station), and of lengths of walls and Roman pottery sherds in Marsa suggest the presence here of port facilities at least since Roman times. Before the annexation of the Maltese islands to Rome in 218 BC, however, when the islands were settled by Phoenician merchants from the eastern Mediterranean and from Carthage, the areas round the south rim of the Grand Harbour seem to have been chosen for settlement. A cemetery of rock-cut tombs discovered along Wied Blandun in Għajn Dwieli over the years point to a settlement that existed here at least from the fifth century BC, living off the agricultural produce from the fertile valley and the marine resources close by.

During the Great Siege of 1565 and again during the Anglo-Maltese blockade of the French in 1798-1800, batteries were established on the Kordin highlands from where attacks were launched on the Senglea peninsula opposite. Excepting the construction of the Knights' powder arsenal on the shore at Ras Ħanżir in 1756, it seems that settlement activity was curtailed on the Kordin heights and the area was transformed into

hunting grounds for the Order of St John. In 1831 the highlands above the powder arsenal were chosen to erect an obelisk in memory of Sir Robert Cavendish Spencer. But when it was realised that the prominence of the mausoleum was prejudicial to harbour defences by enabling enemy warships to take their bearings from it, in 1893 the monument was carted away stone by stone to Blata l-Bajda where it stands to this day.

Permanent changes to the landscape occurred during the British period (1800-1964). With the first

A map depicting the Tukish army in action on Kordin heights during the Great Siege of 1565

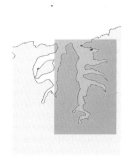

steamship entering Grand Harbour in July 1825, coal was required for bunkering and re-export. Over the years, wharves, coal stores, magazines and storehouses were built by and for the Admiralty along the northern and eastern shores of the Kordin promontory. Vessels in quarantine could now be brought close for ship repair services. A water reservoir was built in 1841 right across the valley behind the Knights' powder arsenal blocking the access route that had linked the coast to the Kordin heights, forcing the authorities to construct a path in its place. Several oil tanks, both above and below ground were also built up until the Second World War. Plans to build a new town on Kordin had started in 1856 but this was blocked by the War Department in 1871 when it was thought that the scheme would jeopardize the Dockyard defences from a landward attack. For this purpose the Kordin entrenchment was built between 1871 and 1880. This consisted of a deep trench stretching

from Ras Ħanżir to Għajn Dwieli, protected by musketry galleries and artillery casemates. Parts of the entrenchment, sadly in need of restoration and maintenance, can still be seen today.

Post-Independence Malta saw the last phase of change to the Kordin landscape. In 1975 work started on a new dock (No 6, China Dock) along several wharves in French Creek. This entailed a lot of rock cutting and demolishing a clutter of buildings and wharves built during the British Period. In 1976 new wharves for containers and RoRo traffic were laid out by the Order's powder magazine, and a road was cut in the rock to link the new quays to Għajn Dwieli. By 1985 a large grain silo was also completed in the vicinity. On Kordin heights, the former naval prisons were ceded to the Maltese government in 1965 and now serve as a covered basketball and volleyball pavilion. The industrial estate that covered the Kordin I and II temples sprung up in the decade that followed.

Monument erected in memory of Sir Robert Cavendish Spencer at the tip of Kordin overlooking Grand Harbour

THE PREHISTORIC TEMPLES AT KORDIN III

HOW OLD IS KORDIN III?

Not all the structures that we see today at Kordin III were built at the same time. They are the result of building alterations undertaken over a period of time. As the result of excavations and of the correlation of the data with those obtained from other prehistoric sites we can now divide the history of Kordin III into at least two periods, covering a span of about six centuries between about 3800 BC (Mġarr phase) and 3200 BC (end of Ġgantija phase). The retrieval of pottery of the Tarxien phase from the site suggests a third period possibly lasting until 2500 BC.

The earliest structures belonging to the first period dating from about 3800 BC could include some of the traces of elliptical rooms and enclosures that we see today behind the temples. The note of hesitation here is due to the fact that excavations did not provide sufficient proof to link these structures with the earliest pottery. It is hoped that further work on site could provide more clues about this possibility.

The discovery of pottery of the Mġarr phase from amidst the ruins of Kordin I and II suggests that a village existed here as well, but how much of the constructions that survived until early last century belonged to this phase is, again, impossible to tell.

The second period saw the erection of the Kordin III twin temples on site, a phenomenon that occurred at different scales all over the Maltese islands but notably at Ġgantija in Gozo where the earliest temple goes back to the phase named after that site. At Tarxien, south of Kordin beyond Wied Blandun, the first of a series of four temples was built at this time but here a five-apse plan was chosen instead of the standard trefoil. Moreover, communal burial of the temple builders started at the Ħal Saflieni hypogeum nearby. It is not possible to say which of the two temples at Kordin III is earlier, and a

Architectural development at Kordin III

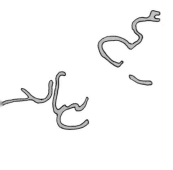

Period 1: Mġarr phase

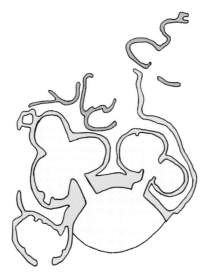

Period 2: Ġgantija phase

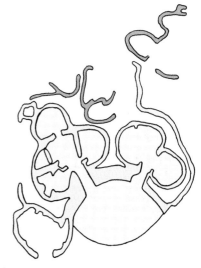

Period 3: Tarxien phase

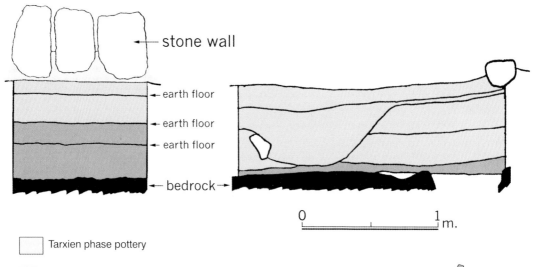

stone wall

← earth floor

← earth floor

← earth floor

← bedrock →

0   1 m.

■ Tarxien phase pottery

■ Ġgantija phase pottery

■ Żebbuġ/Mġarr phase pottery

**Sections showing
archaeological
layers in Trench C
at Kordin III**

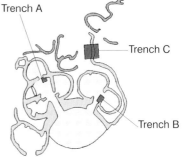

Trench A

Trench C

Trench B

developmental sequence starting with the irregular two-apsed eastern temple followed by the three-apsed, or trefoil, western temple is a hypothetical possibility.

Kordin III is not the only prehistoric site that had grandiose constructions built near or over huts of an earlier date. At the site of Skorba near Żebbiegħ in northern Malta, David Trump demonstrated this transition very clearly by excavation. He was also able to show that the apses of the trefoil temple were cut off from the central court during the Tarxien phase, about 3000 BC: the end apse was walled off, the apse on the left was given a step and the right-hand apse had a screen built above a newly-inserted step. Trump believes that the same probably happened at the western temple at Kordin III, with the 'trough' as an exceptional element inserted in the cross-wall of the left-hand apse. The eastern temple shows no alterations to its interior division.

The dates for Kordin III have been obtained through the combination of two methods. The first method carried out by John Evans in 1953 and by David Trump in 1960, was to make sure that the pottery fragments – with their characteristic shapes and decoration – from Kordin III fitted in the ordered sequence of diagnostic prehistoric pottery from other prehistoric sites in Malta. Ashby's excavations had produced four hundred boxes of pottery but in 1953 Dr Evans could trace only a small portion in the stores of the Museum in Valletta. Three small trenches were dug in different parts of Kordin III in order to check the sequence. One of these (Trench A) entailed the temporary removal of a paving slab in the central court of the western temple. The pottery recovered here, and thus sealed by the temple's paved floor, belonged exclusively to the Ġgantija phase. Similarly, a trench (B) dug in the floor of the eastern temple recovered only Ġgantija phase pottery sherds from a layer that extended below, and was therefore sealed by, the threshold stone in the doorway. Since no sherds of a later phase than Ġgantija turned up in these trenches, the archaeologists concluded that the date of construction would have to be fixed in this phase.

A trench (C) was also dug in a small area between the temples and the rooms or enclosures to the north, but not related physically to any of the surviving walls. Ġgantija phase pottery occurred in a layer above Mġarr phase pottery which in turn rested on bedrock. This has suggested to archaeologists the existence of earlier structures on site, before the temples were built in the Ġgantija phase.

To obtain absolute dates for the successive phases, the same archaeologists resorted to the calibrated results obtained by the radiocarbon process, which can measure the age in calendar years of specimens of animal or vegetable material found in excavations, usually in the form of wood charcoal and animal bones. The organic specimens did not come from Kordin III but from layers with corresponding Ġgantija and Mġarr phase pottery recovered from trenches dug at other prehistoric temple sites on the islands.

Development of prehistoric pottery styles over time. Individual styles are named after the prehistoric site where they were first found

Period		Style	Date
NEOLITHIC	Temple Period	Saflieni	3300-3000 BC
		Ġgantija	3600-3200 BC
		Mġarr	3800-3600 BC
		Żebbuġ	4100-3700 BC
	Early settlers	Red Skorba	4400-4100 BC
		Grey Skorba	4500-4400 BC
		Għar Dalam	5000-4300 BC

BEDROCK

The idea of prehistory

The approximate date of the temples that we see at Kordin III is only the result of recent archaeological work and scientific studies. Up until the eighteenth century, it was still believed that giants were the original inhabitants of the Maltese islands. Indeed, Gian Francesco Abela, Vice-Chancellor of the Order of St John, writing in 1647 in his *Della Descrittione di Malta*, suggested that huge fossil bones could be associated with some of the islands' great megalithic ruins. In the nineteenth century naturalists and fossil hunters who visited Malta realized that these giant bones and teeth belonged to large mammals long extinct. Myths of giants and diluvial theories soon gave way to more plausible tales involving the Phoenicians in order to explain the megalithic phenomenon in the Mediterranean. It was only towards the end of the century that differences between the architecture of the Phoenicians in their Levantine homeland and the megalithic buildings of Malta were recognized. Human presence in Malta had to be far older than the Phoenicians, indeed older than the period of the earliest written documents. With no objects of bronze or iron having been found in any of the Maltese megalithic temples investigated until then, including Kordin III, it was logical to assume that they belonged to the Stone Age. An idea of prehistory gradually took shape as archaeological digging techniques improved and science, especially the advent of radiocarbon dating, established a firm timescale for the antiquity of humankind.

MALTA'S EARLIEST PREHISTORIC SETTLERS

By the time that people decided to settle on the Kordin promontory, Malta had been inhabited by human groups who practised an early form of farming for more than a thousand years. The earliest settlers almost certainly came from Sicily to the north, across 90 km of open sea, about 5000 BC. Successful, perhaps storm-driven, voyages appear to have been numerous enough to populate the islands, and the sea-craft were of a type that could carry animals as well as humans. In any event, the ability of these ancient seafarers to make crossings and survive at sea defies our modern urban imagination.

These first settlers brought with them the know-how to shape and fire clay, locally available, in order to make pottery containers. The dark, polished pottery has a characteristic impressed decoration invariably filled with a white paste. The style is that of contemporary sites in south-east Sicily and was first found in Malta at Għar Dalam, a cave in the side of the valley that runs down to Marsaxlokk Bay. In the following centuries, up until the Mġarr phase about 3800 BC when the high grounds at Kordin attracted humans to settle on, the pottery styles followed closely those on eastern Sicily and the Aeolian islands to the north. In the Mġarr phase, the pottery being produced was of a harder quality. The decoration is now gouged out, running vertically along the body of the pot down from the rim, sometimes interspersed with light scratches or fringes. White paste was still applied but this was given a wash with ground red ochre powder, a mineral that occurs naturally in Sicily, from where it was imported.

The earliest settlers cultivated primitive cereals and kept domesticated animals such as sheep,

Islands give many signs of their existence, besides being visible. The orographic rain clouds that tower above the Maltese islands are often visible long before the islands come in sight

goats, cattle, and dogs, their remains having been discovered in pre-temple layers at the village of Skorba. Carbonized grains of barley, wheat, and lentils were recovered too. For shelter, people sought natural caves, such as Għar Dalam itself and the cave at Għajn Għabdun in western Gozo, but they built huts as well, their existence surmised from the traces of a hut floor made of clay and pebbles also at Skorba. Huts of the later Red Skorba phase are not very different, being roughly oval in shape with massive stone footings round the perimeter for a superstructure of mud brick. A preference for properly laid-out *torba* floors is, however, perceptible. Some of the *torba* uncovered at Kordin III in the area behind the temples, covered with, and containing pottery of the Mġarr phase, could belong to similar huts. The clay that Ashby identified could represent the use of mud brick for a superstructure, likely to have been obtained from a nearby alluvial plain or valley bottom rather than from the distant exposures of blue clay in the north-west of the island.

For tools and hunting weapons, these early settlers used stone that could be worked into desired shapes with a cutting edge. On the Maltese islands, only chert was available in local outcrops of Globigerina limestone, to be fashioned, with difficulty, into sharp tools. More popular because of its hard and brittle characteristics was flint, obtained from the Hyblaean hills in the hinterland of Syracuse in Sicily. But far superior to either for its flaking qualities was obsidian, a black volcanic glass brought to the Maltese islands from Lipari to the north of Sicily or from Pantelleria to the north-west of Malta. At Skorba, lumps or cores of obsidian were discovered ready to be hit – knapped is the technical word – by a skilled person to detach flakes of desired

Caves have been used for habitation since prehistoric times. Here farmers stand outside their caves at Fawwara, Malta (c.1900) where animals were penned.

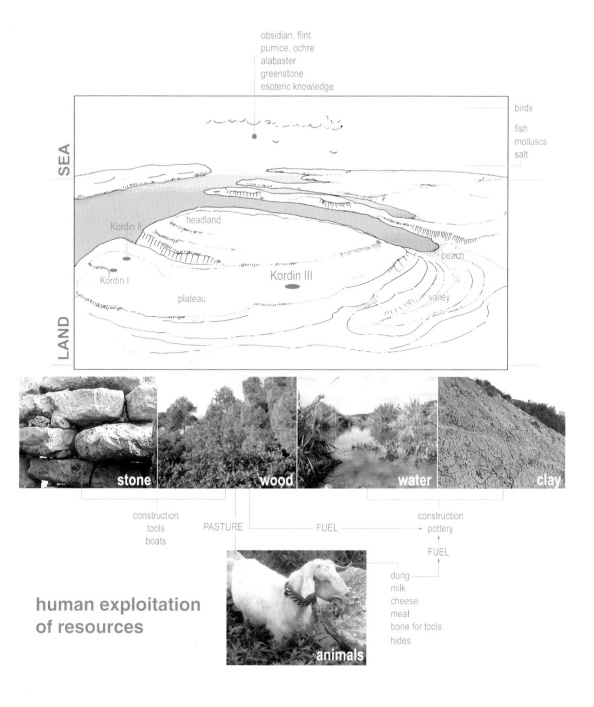

obsidian, flint
pumice, ochre
alabaster
greenstone
esoteric knowledge

birds
fish
molluscs
salt

SEA

LAND

Kordin II
headland
Kordin I
Kordin III
plateau
beach
valley

stone   wood   water   clay

construction
tools   PASTURE   FUEL   construction
boats   pottery

                                                FUEL

dung
milk
cheese
meat
bone for tools
hides

human exploitation
of resources

animals

shape. Scrapers for cleaning animal hides, blades for cutting up meat or for butchering, burins and awls for making holes in hides, and arrowheads as projectile points were produced by retouching the edges of the flakes, perhaps using antler horns imported from Sicily. Examples of such tools were found at Kordin III but since they seem to be associated with the temple builders reference to them should better be left for the section that follows.

MALTA'S TEMPLE BUILDERS

About 3600 BC, events in the Maltese islands took a singular turn. For the next millennium, the landscape witnessed substantial cultural changes and developments. Neolithic farmers probably grew in numbers and labour could now be spared for communal works. Large megalithic structures were built throughout both islands, small at first but becoming bigger, complex structures over time, involving a motley crew of skilled specialists probably working under the leadership of a master mason. We can refer to these constructions as 'temples' for the time being, as we have been doing so far, but we shall return to this intriguing issue shortly. Before doing so, it would be good to have a wider look at life during the Temple Period.

The knowledge we have of daily life is limited for the simple reason that only a few domestic sites have so far been located and excavated. From what remained of the Ġgantija phase oval hut that was excavated in 1987 near the Għajnsielem plain in Gozo,

we can surmise that dwelling fashions and construction methods remained unaltered from earlier periods. Pottery was still being made, with some exceptionally fine wares making their appearance for the first time, some plain in black and grey fabrics but the majority decorated with incised spirals and converging curves. One pot reached gargantuan proportions, 85 cm across at the rim. From Kordin III, Ashby's team lifted a large number of crates of pottery, some of which were reconstructed into near-complete pots when the museum stores were being reorganized by Evans in the 1950s. Deep open bowls with scratched decoration typical of the Ġgantija phase are represented together with a Saflieni phase bowl with a handle. Miniature pots of the same shape with criss-cross designs were recovered too. A large narrow-necked jar with two horizontal tubular handles and two vertically pierced string-hole lugs below the neck is unique in Ġgantija phase contexts in Malta. Its scratched decoration filled with red paste depicts what appear to be a series of boats.

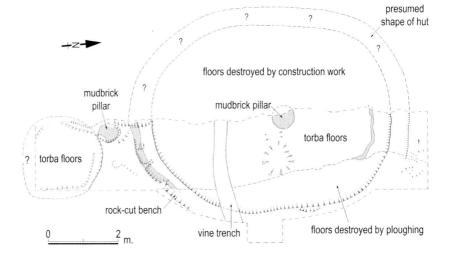

The oval plan for domestic huts was kept thoughout Maltese prehistory as is seen in this example excavated by the Mġarr Road, Għajnsielem, Gozo

The ubiquitous carinated bowl of the Tarxien phase is also represented at Kordin III, an imposing example 48 cm across at the rim. Another carinated bowl of the same phase shows two decorative techniques, the part above the carination being covered in lozenge-shaped pits that were subsequently inlaid with white paste, and below the carination decorated with wild curves and spirals in broad incision, afterwards filled with white paste too.

If incisions on pots could have been produced by pointed bone implements, those on stone, in low or high relief, inside the temples had to be produced by stone tools. Cutting edges were still being produced by chert, flint, and obsidian, implying that overseas trading connections with Sicily and its islands, directly or indirectly, still flourished well into the Tarxien phase. A fine flint arrowhead, with characteristic short barbs, was recovered in 1908 from Kordin I, together with scrapers of poor flint or chert.

Much more is known about 'life' in the Temple Period through the burial rituals. These were of a communal sort with bodies, both male and female and sometimes accompanied by domestic animals, being buried in underground hypogea. The rites involved the stacking of disarticulated bones when space within the chambers or pits was limited. Ceramic vessels, beads, bone and stone tools, amulets and pendants made of imported green stone, but also intricate anthromorphic and zoomorphic figurines and statues were all items – gifts – buried with the dead. From the ongoing study of the bones unearthed from the Xagħra hypogeum in Gozo (also known to archaeologists as the Brochtorff Circle or the Xagħra Stone Circle) a picture emerges of the temple builders: they were stockily built and of medium height, accustomed to walking on hard ground; they had few health problems apparently beyond the discomfort and pain caused by arthritis and dental abscesses.

A modern piece of obsidian from Lipari

About 200 lithic tools were recovered from Kordin I

Reconstructed Ġgantija phase amphora (right) and reconstructed Tarxien phase carinated bowl from Kordin III

An obsidian blade from Kordin photographed against light to enhance the translucent nature of the material

WHAT WENT ON INSIDE THE TEMPLES?

This question is a difficult one. In our attempt to answer it will we assume that we share the same definition of a temple with Malta's prehistoric settlers, that it is a special building set aside for the practice of religious ritual. Since no written sources have come down to us from the period of the temples, this intriguing question has to be answered solely on the basis of the form of the megalithic monuments themselves and the archaeological remains recovered within. First, the form of the monuments. The majority of the temples, Kordin III included, all have the same organic shape, based on a combination of lobed spaces or apses, added to over a period lasting about seven centuries. In all there is a clear distinction between the inside and outside, the curvilinear façade with its deep doorway and threshold directing movement but acting as a boundary between the forecourt and the internal lobed areas. Raised sills across the doorway in the western temple at Kordin mark the entrance, hindering symbolically rather than physically, passage into the building. Inside the monument, inner recesses are closed off by steps and screens and by the large 'trough' that lies to one side of the central court. There appears to be a clear attempt to mark entrances and exits and to control and direct the movement of those that were allowed inside to particular areas. The posture of people was being conditioned by the architectural layout and so was their experience. Similar formality in the layout of buildings is often encountered in churches and cathedrals where people are allowed access to certain areas and not others, and where they are made to behave in particular ways during the enactment of religious rituals. But other rituals, of a secular and social rather than religious type, can dictate the layout of a building. A football stadium, for instance, has areas that define where those taking part in the game – players or spectators – should stay. The same can be said of an auditorium or theatre.

Size matters: portability could relate to the function of prehistoric images

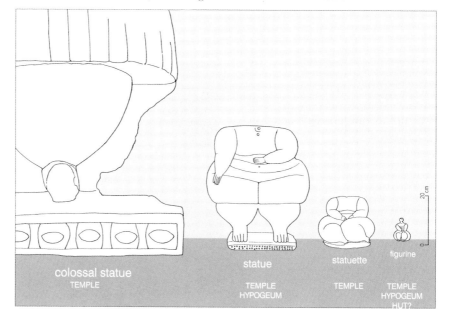

colossal statue
TEMPLE

statue
TEMPLE
HYPOGEUM

statuette
TEMPLE

figurine
TEMPLE
HYPOGEUM
HUT?

20 cm

THE PREHISTORIC TEMPLES AT KORDIN III

As a criterion, therefore, the form of the monuments is not enough to answer our question. What remains to be seen is whether the objects and furniture recovered from the megalithic monuments could have been used in connection with actions directed to a divine or supernatural being. It is difficult to make a case for Kordin III taken in complete isolation, but when viewed with other sites, especially Tarxien nearby, the matter is significantly altered. Besides form, the main common feature linking the major megalithic monuments of Malta together is the presence within them of images of the human figure. Sitting, squatting, and standing, with one or both hands on the abdomen, sculpted in stone or moulded in clay, for the most part asexual, the statuettes and the figurines have a significance that accompanied the temple builders in life and in death. At Tarxien, a colossal statue of a standing human figure that comes into view as soon as one enters the western temple has a unique status in the entire complex in terms both of scale and of workmanship. This easily makes the personage the best candidate for a representation of a deity, and the smaller ones that occur at Tarxien and elsewhere – now on display at the National Museum of Archaeology in Valletta – as multiple representations of the same deity or votive offerings rather than votaries. Were it not for the asexual nature of the majority of the figures, a belief in a mother goddess would be plausible. Or would it? Could the colossal statue not be a representation of a high-ranking ancestor – male or female – deified perhaps, called upon by the temple builders to help them in times of change? As so often in archaeology,

no single explanation will suffice. Whoever is being represented, however, seems to have been acknowledged by acts of worship that involved offerings. In the room where the colossal statue occurs, a platform decorated with spirals in relief probably acted as an altar or offering table. A flint knife and a goat's horn were found deep inside a cubby-hole on its front, and animal bones were piled behind it. The deep bowl that was found in large quantities at Tarxien as well as at other temple sites, including Kordin III, was probably used for such rituals, containing food or liquid gifts. Feasting, a powerful social unifier, could have been an important part of the ritual. But whether everyone was allowed to take part and to proceed inside the temples from the forecourt outside, rather than remaining there, is hard to tell.

For Kordin III, it would be stretching the evidence too far to propose more than we have done so far. No significant alignments with the celestial bodies are apparent for the temples either other than the preferred southerly orientation. No statuettes or figurines were recovered from this site, neither as far as we know from its partners on the Kordin

This reconstructed Tarxien phase bowl from Kordin III could have been used for food or liquid offerings inside the temples

The 'trough' as it appeared soon after Ashby's excavations in 1909

promontory. It could be that at the close of the Temple Period, the monumental multi-temple complex at Tarxien eclipsed its neighbours in importance, becoming the focus of rituals for an entire district or region. What is intriguing, for the simple reason that nothing like it has been found elsewhere on Malta and Gozo, is the 'trough' of the western temple at Kordin III. It is generally assumed by archaeologists that this is a communal quern for grinding grain, perhaps to mark the harvest, an interpretation that is telling considering that the temples overlook the fertile Wied Blandun, undoubtedly a source of food in prehistory. But archaeologist Reuben Grima has recently returned to Ashby's original definition of the

worked block as 'boat-like', suggesting that the 'trough' could actually mimic a prehistoric boat with bulkheads. Placed inside a religious monument located not far from the sea, this model of a boat – both receptacle and threshold – could have invoked the movement of people and exchanges across the sea. Those that travelled by boat beyond the horizon, clearly visible from the Kordin promontory, acquired knowledge of extraordinary things and matters removed from mundane everyday life. Such esoteric knowledge may have been harnessed by some to express power and authority over those that had never travelled, those that had not seen what was beyond the horizon. Kordin III could have been a repository of such knowledge, a place where knowledge traditions about the world were assembled.

In any case, temples were built on the Kordin promontory in a location that falls between the sea and agricultural land. In his excavation report of 1896, Dr A. A. Caruana had made a remark about this explicit connection between the coast and the megalithic temples. Nowadays, with most visitors approaching the island at the end of a flight lasting not more than a few hours at most, just over half-an-hour if the aeroplane takes off from Sicily, this link might not be apparent at all. Those who arrive in Grand Harbour on board a luxury liner, or take a boat cruise, are a step closer to a mode of transport prevalent in prehistory and can appreciate the affinity with the sea that the temples, placed on a coastal promontory, would have had.

We invite you to take a boat trip round the harbour, hoping that this guide will have served to whet your appetite for knowing more about Malta's intriguing prehistoric temples.

Detail of boat graffiti on reconstructed amphora

GLOSSARY

amphora A large two-handled ceramic jar with narrow neck and pointed or rounded base.

anthropomorphic In art, referring to a visual representation based on the appearance or characteristics of humans.

apses A word used to denote the horseshoe-shaped rooms that usually face each other on either side of a corridor or court in the prehistoric temples of Malta.

bedrock Undisturbed natural substrate below any archaeological deposits; in the Maltese context the bedrock is solid rock.

carinated A term often applied to a ceramic bowl with an almost vertical upper wall above a sharp inward change of direction (the carination).

chert A flint-like material that occurs as nodules in limestone, even in Malta; used in prehistory to make tools but does not lend itself to fine working like flint and obsidian.

entrenchment A position fortified by trenches.

escarpment The precipitous side of a hill, ridge, or promontory.

esoteric knowledge Knowledge of things that are beyond the familiar everyday world, usually those that are to be found in geographically distant places.

flint A hard brittle siliceous rock forming in chalk or limestone that is highly suitable for the manufacture of edged tools by knapping; the nearest source of flint was the limestone Hyblaean mountain range in south-east Sicily.

hypogeum A rock-cut chambered tomb with a series of interlinking rooms.

lintel A horizontal stone placed over a doorway or window; in prehistoric temple architecture the lintel is placed above two or more megaliths flanking an entrance.

lug (lug handle) A lump of solid clay that protrudes from the wall of a pot to facilitate handling

megalith Literally, a big stone (from the Greek *megas*, 'large', and *lithos*, 'stone').

Neolithic Literally, New Stone Age (from the Greek *neos*, 'new', and *lithos*, 'stone'), as opposed to Palaeolithic or older Stone Age; a period of prehistory associated with the beginnings of farming when societies depended on raising crops and domesticated animals for their subsistence.

obsidian A naturally occurring black volcanic glass extensively used in the production of edged tools; in the central Mediterranean sources are known in the islands of Lipari, Pantelleria, Palmarola, and Sardinia.

ochre Oxides of iron in yellow or red forms that occur naturally, though not in Malta, often used in prehistory as a colouring material and also for spreading on corpses during death rituals.

orthostat Large upstanding stone used in constructing the walls of the prehistoric temples.

promontory An eminent ridge or headland usually overlooking the sea.

radiocarbon dating A technique for determining the absolute date of organic matter based on the fact that all living organisms contain a small but constant proportion of the radioactive isotope of carbon, ^{14}C. When the organism dies the ^{14}C is no longer replenished from the environment and what is present at the time of death decays at a known constant rate. By measuring the radioactivity of the carbon remaining in a specimen its age can be calculated.

radiocarbon calibration The adjustment of radiocarbon dates for the effect of variation in ^{14}C carried out by using curves on a chart obtained from tree-ring chronologies.

topography The detailed description of the landform and geographical features of the landscape of an area.

torba The Maltese word for a hard plaster-like material made by the repeated pounding and wetting of several layers of Globigerina limestone dust; it was usually spread over a rubble foundation for making temple and hut floors.

typology The classification of objects (e.g. pottery) into a sequence or series of groups (types) and subgroups (subtypes); for prehistoric Malta the pottery series is made of groups of pots named after the prehistoric site where they were first found.

zoomorphic In art referring to a visual representation based on the appearance or characteristics of an animal.

FURTHER READING

In square brackets are indicated the libraries where out-of-print or hard-to-get publications can be consulted in Malta: NLM = National Library of Malta (Pjazza Regina, Valletta; www.libraries-archives.gov.mt, (+356) 21 243297; UOM = Melitensia section, University of Malta Library (Tal-Qroqq campus, Msida; www.lib.um.edu.mt, (+356) 2340 2049).

The nineteenth-century archaeological explorations on the Kordin promontory are recorded in C. Vassallo's *Dei monumenti antichi del gruppo di Malta* (Malta, 1876) [NLM] and in A. A. Caruana's 'Further megalithic discoveries and exploration in the island of Malta during 1892 and 1893 under the Governorship of Sir Henry A. Smyth, K.C.M.G.' published in the *Archaeological Journal* 53 (1896) [NLM]. T. Ashby and his colleagues reported their excavation at Kordin III in the *Papers of the British School at Rome* 6/1 (1913): 1-126. J. D. Evans excavated a trench at Kordin III in 1953 and studied the pottery from the Ashby excavations; his results are published in the seminal volume *Prehistoric Antiquities of the Maltese Islands, a survey* (London, 1970) [NLM, UOM] to which the reader is directed for detail about Kordin and other prehistoric sites. D. Trump enlarged the same trench and published his observations on chronological issues in the final report for the Skorba excavations, *Skorba* (London, 1966).

On the changing landscape of the Kordin promontory and the Grand Harbour area generally, the book by J. Bonnici and M. Cassar, *The Malta Grand Harbour and its Dockyard* (Malta, 1994) is useful, especially the extensive illustrations. The eighteenth-century discovery of alleged Roman warehouses at the foot of Jesuits Hill in Marsa by Count A. Barbaro are reported in *Degli avanzi d'alcuni antichissimi edifizi, scoperti a Malta l'anno 1768* (Malta, 1794) [NLM]. The excavation report of the Punic tombs found at Għajn Dwieli along Wied Blandun was published by J. D. Baldacchino in the *Papers of the British School at Rome* 19 (1951) [UOM]. Details of the Kordin entrenchment are to be sought in Stephen Spiteri's *British Military Architecture in Malta* (Malta, 1996).

For excellent updated surveys on Maltese prehistory that help to set Kordin III in a wider context, both spatial and temporal, the reader is directed to D. Trump's *Malta, prehistory and temples* (Malta, 2002) and A. Bonanno's *Il-preistorja* (Malta, 2002).

Ideas on the interpretation and meaning of prehistoric art, including the finds from the Xagħra Stone Circle, have been gathered by A. Pace in an exhibition catalogue entitled *Prehistoric Art in Malta, 5000-2500 BC* (Malta, 1996). The importance of scale and portability in order to understand prehistoric imagery has been stressed by A. Townsend in an article he co-authored with C. Malone and S. Stoddart in an elusive journal published in the Netherlands, *Caecvlvs* 2 (1995) [UOM]. R. Grima's suggestion that the "trough" from Kordin III could represent a model of a prehistoric sea vessel have been put forth in an insightful article, 'An iconography of insularity: a cosmological interpretation of some images and spaces in the Late Neolithic temples of Malta' published in the *Papers from the Institute of Archaeology* 12 (2001), 48-65 [NLM, UOM]. J. Robb's 'Island identities: ritual, travel and the creation of difference in Neolithic Malta' published in the *Journal of European Archaeology* 4/2 (2001): 175-202 [UOM], argues against Malta's insularity at the end of the Temple period.

Finally, the idea that the temples could be seen as "depositories of knowledge" is from D. Turnbull's 'Performance and narrative, bodies and movement in the construction of places and objects, spaces and knowledges: the case of the Maltese megaliths', published in *Theory, Culture and Society* 19 (2002) [UOM].